Copyright 2020 - by Beth Costanzo

In this latest exploration of some of our planet's most fascinating animals, I wanted to focus on an animal that is close to us. It has so many similarities with humans because it is a primate.

Here, I am talking about the

ORANGUTAN

Orangutans are some of the most interesting creatures in our animal kingdom. They are smart, resourceful, and have been on our planet for millions of years. While you will likely see an orangutan in a zoo, you may be quite lucky and see a real-life orangutan in the wild.

So come along with me and explore why the orangutan is so captivating. I'm sure you'll be fascinated!

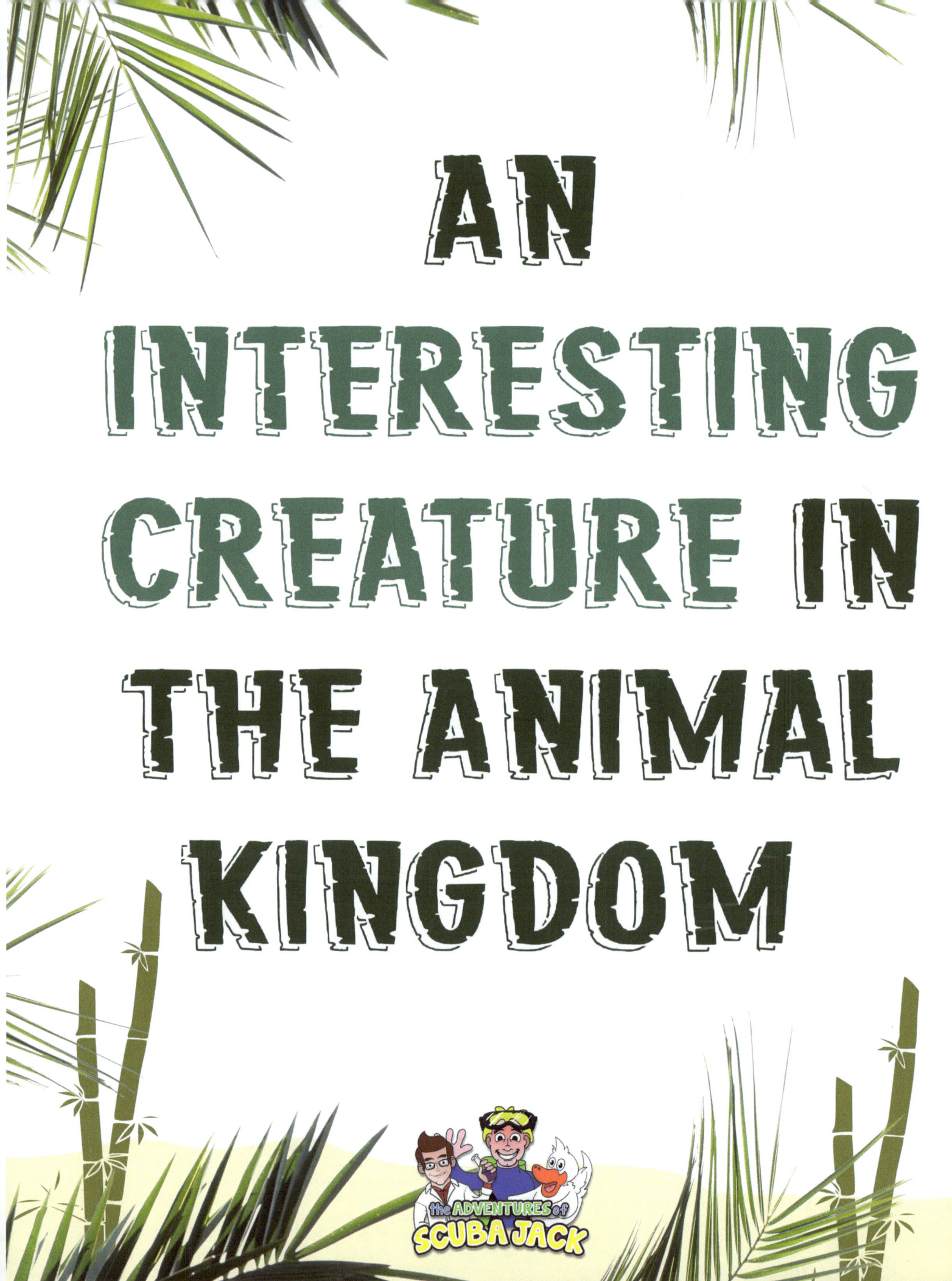

To start, one of the most interesting things about orangutans is their appearance. These animals have a famous reddish-brown color and a face that looks remarkably human. While their faces don't have much hair on them, some orangutans can even have little mustaches!

Besides their faces, orangutans have large bodies. Females are around three feet, nine inches tall and weigh around 80 pounds. Males are around four feet, six inches tall and weigh around 165 pounds. To get around, orangutans walk on their fists. This is different from chimpanzees and gorillas (they walk on their knuckles). Orangutan hands are very similar to human hands. They have four fingers and a thumb (just like you), but their fingers are long and their thumb is much shorter. Their hands let them travel in the treeline.

Another important feature of the orangutan is its intelligence. It's hard to find a smarter primate in the animal kingdom. One of the most interesting things about their intelligence is that orangutans are known to use tools. These tools help them accomplish tasks throughout their day. For example, orangutans use tools to help them construct nests where they can sleep. Some orangutans have even used tools to help them with communication.

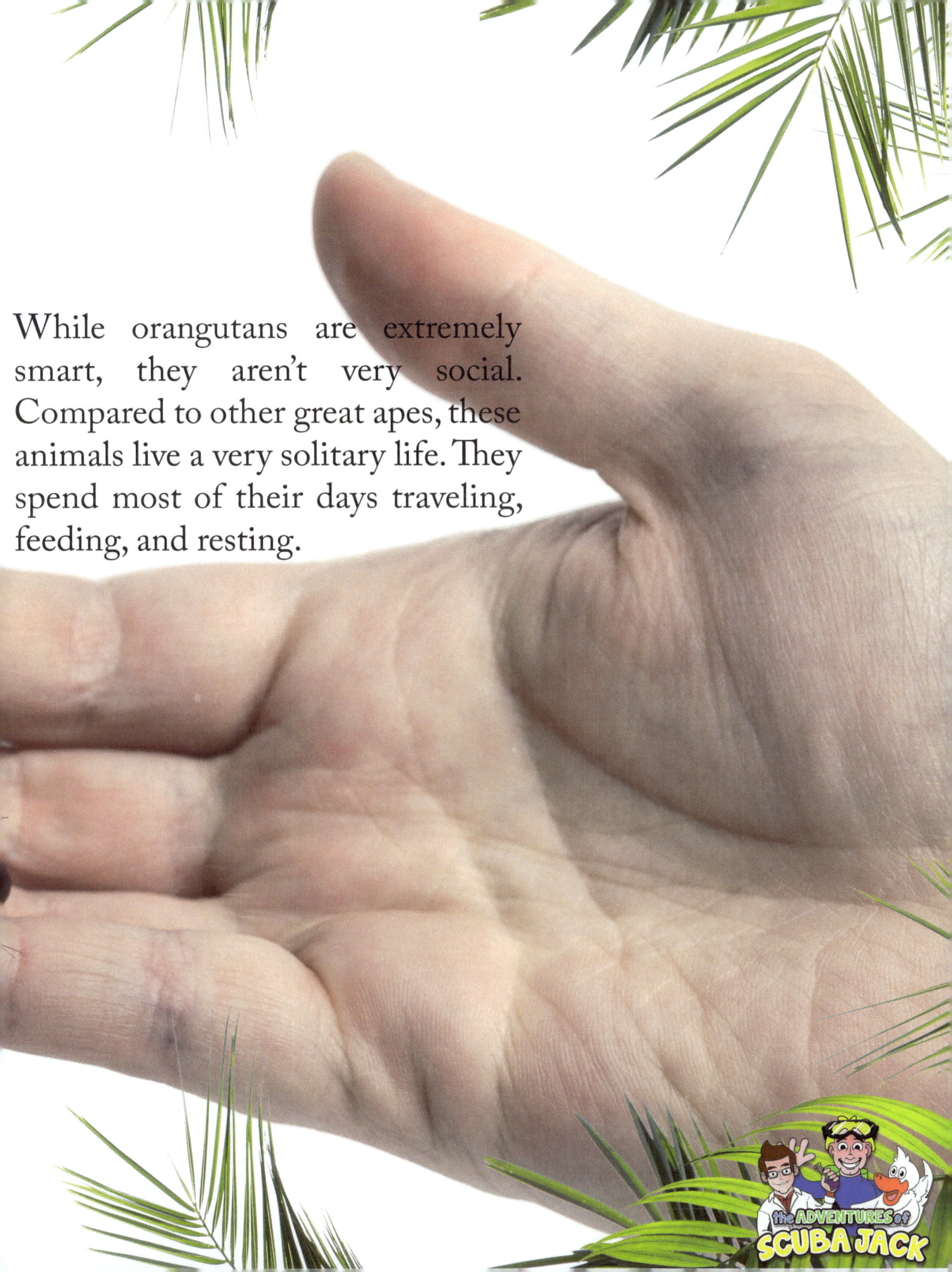

While orangutans are extremely smart, they aren't very social. Compared to other great apes, these animals live a very solitary life. They spend most of their days traveling, feeding, and resting.

Orangutans have been on our planet for an extremely long time. In fact, scientists who have looked at old orangutan fossils believe that the first orangutan walked Earth around two million years ago. Since then, the orangutan has evolved into the animal that we know and love. Originally, scientists thought that there were only two species of orangutans. However, in November 2017, scientists identified a third species of orangutan in Indonesia.

Many orangutans are found in forests, but they can also be found in mountains or low swampy areas. In the wild, they can only be found in two countries (Indonesia and Malaysia). While they used to live in China and some Southeast Asian countries, you'll need to travel to Indonesia or Malaysia to catch a glimpse of them in their natural habitat.

As for its diet, orangutans eat lots of fruit. It comes out to be around 65 to 90 percent of the orangutan's diet. But along with this extremely important food, orangutans like to munch on things like bark, honey, vegetation, insects, and bird eggs. Because orangutans spend lots of time in trees, they tend to find lots of their food above the ground.

BABY ORANGUTANS

With this basic understanding of orangutans in mind, let's go on to something really cute—*the baby orangutan*.

Female orangutans have their first children when they are about 14 or 15 years old. These female orangutans give birth about once every eight years. Mothers often give birth to one baby at a time, but there are some exceptions.

When they are born, baby orangutans have wrinkled faces and thin feet and hands. They are also very dependent on their mothers. In fact, for the first two years of their lives, baby orangutans basically can't live without them.

From the time baby orangutans are born to when they are four months old, they are carried on their stomachs. Throughout all of this, they don't lose touch or physical contact with their mothers. As they get older, they rely less on their mothers. At the age of two, these baby orangutans can rely on their new climbing skills. One of the coolest things that these baby orangutans do is hold hands with other orangutans and travel throughout the forest canopy.

Ultimately, these baby orangutans stay with their mothers for around six to seven years. At that time, they weigh about 25 pounds. They have also matured and developed enough skills where they can leave their mothers and live on their own.

MORE FUN FACTS ABOUT ORANGUTANS

The orangutan is one of the most fascinating animals for a reason. It is extremely intelligent and it has been walking our planet for millions of years. Also, compared to other animals, you are going to need to take a long plane ride to see them in the wild. And who could forget how cute their babies are!

TO IMPRESS YOUR FRIENDS AND FAMILY, HERE ARE SOME MORE INTERESTING FACTS ABOUT THE ORANGUTAN.

Orangutans tend to communicate in different ways. For example, males make long calls. When infants are feeling stressed or scared, they make soft hoots. Both males and females even make noises called "rolling calls" to intimidate other orangutans.

Orangutans start their days by eating in the morning. But it isn't just a quick snack. Orangutans spend two to three hours filling their bellies.

These animals follow specific instructions when building their nests. In fact, once younger orangutans can follow the steps and build nests on their end, they typically feel free to leave their mothers.

Zoo Atlanta has a touch-screen computer where orangutans actually play games. This goes to show how smart they are!

Orangutans are endangered. Many organizations are hard at work to make sure they don't go extinct.

Orangutans often travel alone, but they may travel with others before they become adults.

Orangutans don't swim, although some have been spotted carefully wading into water.

Human environmental destruction has caused severe declines in orangutan populations.

ORANGUTANS ACTIVITIES

TRACING

Trace the word below then rewrite it

Orangutan

COUNTING

Count the baby Orangutans and circle the correct answer

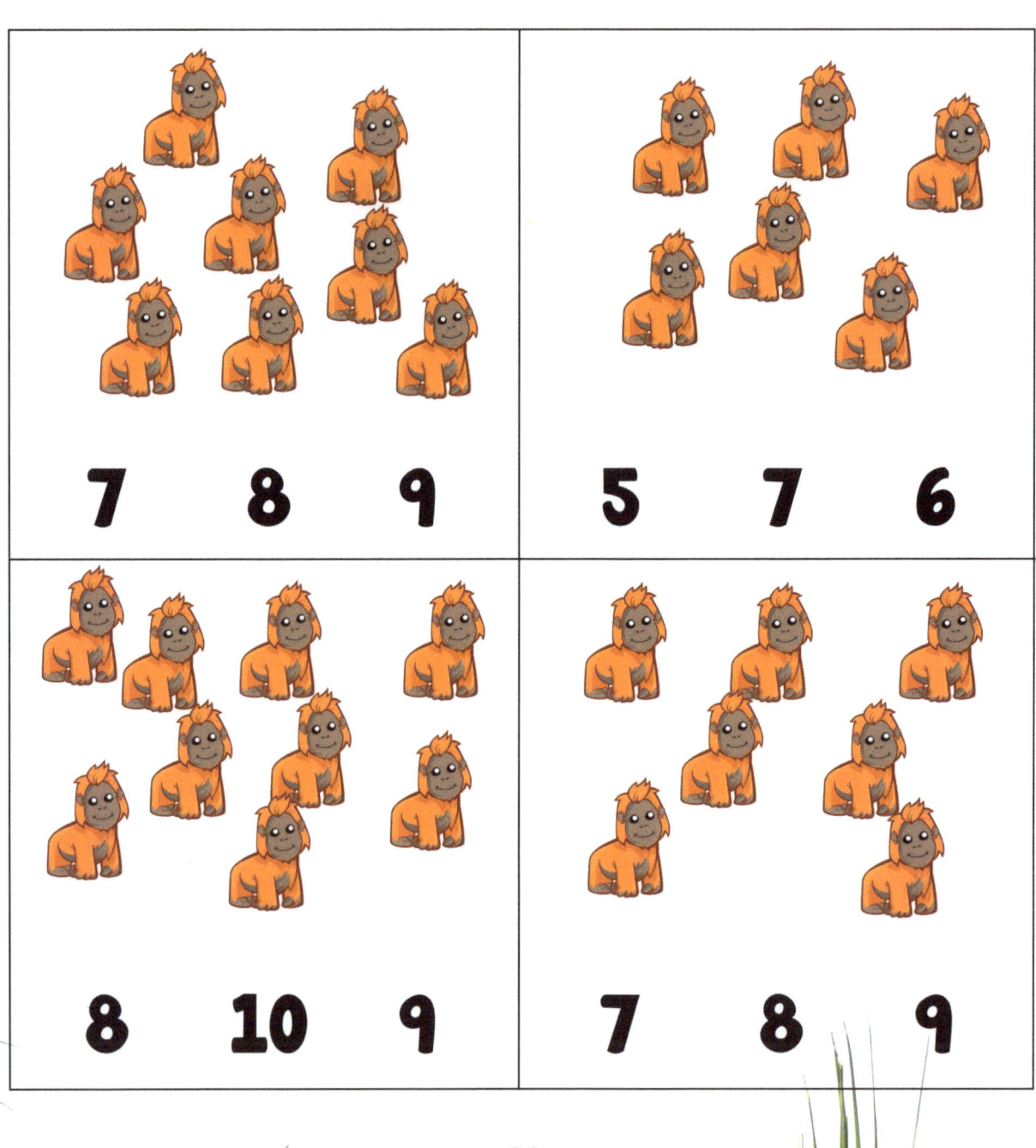

TREE

Trace the Tree then color it so the baby Orangutan don't fall

ORANGUTAN CRAFT

Let's make a cute Orangutan!

You will need:

Scissors
Glue
Coloring Pencils

Directions:

1- Cut the Orangutan's body part, head part, legs & hands
2- Glue hands to the body
3- Glue the legs to the body
4- Glue the head inside the body
5- Color your cute Orangutan!

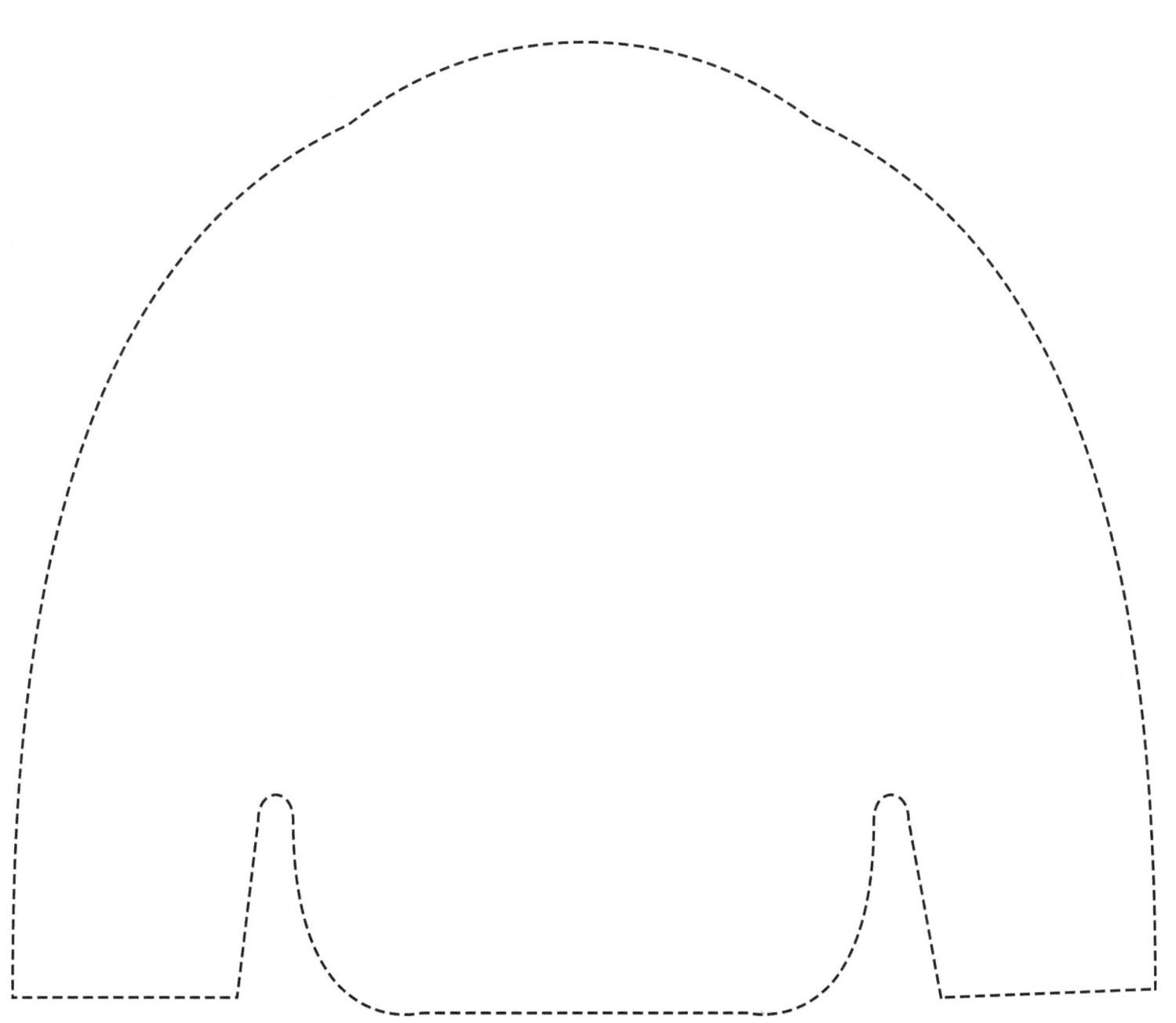

VISIT US AT
WWW.ADVENTURESOFSCUBAJACK.COM

www.ingramcontent.com/pod-product-compliance
Lightning Source LLC
Chambersburg PA
CBHW041435010526
44118CB00002B/81